Brownies
Fudges
and Toppings

KÖNEMANN

Brownies

Indulge in one of these delicious brownies when you are craving something rich and moreish. Your family and friends will love the variety of flavours and textures, from nutty or fruity to chewy and chocolaty. Easy to make, you can have them for morning or afternoon tea or to finish off a meal.

Super Fudge Brownies

Preparation time:
  20 minutes
  + refrigeration
Total cooking time:
  50–55 minutes
Makes 50

200 g (6¹/2 oz) dark
  chocolate, chopped
200 g (6¹/2 oz) butter,
  chopped
4 eggs
1 cup (250 g/8 oz)
  caster sugar
1 teaspoon vanilla
  essence
1¹/3 cups (165 g/
  5¹/2 oz) plain flour
¹/4 cup (30 g/1 oz)
  cocoa powder

1. Preheat the oven to moderate 180°C (350°F/Gas 4). Brush a shallow 20 x 30 cm (8 x 12 inch) tin with oil or melted butter. Line the base with baking paper, extending over the 2 long sides.
2. Melt the chocolate and butter in a large heatproof bowl over a pan of simmering water, stirring occasionally. Remove from the heat and allow to cool slightly.
3. Beat the eggs, sugar and vanilla essence together with a wire whisk until combined. Add to the chocolate mixture with the sifted flour and cocoa. Stir until just combined.
4. Pour into the tin and bake for 45–50 minutes. Allow to cool completely in the tin; refrigerate for 2–3 hours, until firm. Cut into small squares. Can be decorated with icing or melted chocolate and icing flowers.

Super Fudge Brownies

Macadamia Blondies

Preparation time:
  12 minutes + cooling
Total cooking time:
  40–45 minutes
Makes 24

100 g (3¹/3 oz) unsalted
  butter
100 g (3¹/3 oz) white
  chocolate
¹/2 cup (125 g/4 oz)
  caster sugar
2 eggs, lightly beaten
1 teaspoon vanilla
  essence
1 cup (125 g/4 oz)
  self-raising flour
¹/2 cup (80 g/2²/3 oz)
  macadamia nuts,
  roughly chopped

1. Preheat the oven to moderate 180°C (350°F/Gas 4). Brush a 20 cm (8 inch) square tin with oil or melted butter and line the base with baking paper.
2. Melt the butter and the white chocolate in a heatproof bowl, over a pan of simmering water, stirring until smooth. Remove from the heat.
3. Add the caster sugar to the bowl and then gradually stir in the lightly beaten eggs. Add the vanilla, fold in the flour and nuts and then pour the mixture into the prepared tin.

4. Bake for 35–40 minutes. If the top starts to brown too quickly, cover lightly with a sheet of foil. When cooked, remove from the oven and allow to cool in the tin before turning out and cutting into squares. Shown drizzled with melted white chocolate.

Coffee Brownies

Preparation time:
  20 minutes
  + refrigeration
Total cooking time:
  40 minutes
Makes 16

125 g (4 oz) butter
125 g (4 oz) dark
  chocolate
1¹/2 teaspoons instant
  coffee, dissolved
  in 1 teaspoon of
  hot water
¹/2 cup (115 g/3³/4 oz)
  firmly packed soft
  brown sugar
2 eggs, lightly beaten
¹/2 cup (60 g/2 oz)
  self-raising flour
¹/3 cup (40 g/1¹/3 oz)
  chopped pecans

Topping
50 g (1²/3 oz) butter,
  softened to room
  temperature
1¹/2 cups (185 g/6 oz)
  icing sugar

3 teaspoons instant
  coffee, dissolved in
  1 tablespoon of
  boiling water

1. Preheat the oven to moderate 180°C (350°F/Gas 4). Brush a 20 cm (8 inch) square tin with melted butter or oil and line the base with baking paper.
2. Melt the butter and chocolate in a heatproof bowl over a pan of simmering water, stirring until smooth. Add the coffee and sugar and stir until the sugar has almost dissolved. Remove from the heat.
3. Beat in the eggs and a pinch of salt. Fold in the flour and pecans; pour into the tin. Bake for 25 minutes, then cool a little in the tin.
4. *To make Topping:* Beat together the butter and the icing sugar; add the dissolved coffee. The mixture should be of spreading consistency — add a little more water if necessary.
5. While the brownie mixture is still warm, turn out of the tin and spread or dot with Topping. Refrigerate for 10 minutes, or until Topping is firm. Cut into diamonds. Shown decorated with chocolate icing and coffee beans.

Coffee Brownies (top) and Macadamia Blondies

Caramel Brownies

Preparation time:
  15 minutes + cooling
Total cooking time:
  35–40 minutes
Makes 16

1/2 cup (60 g/2 oz)
  self-raising flour
1/3 cup (40 g/1 1/3 oz)
  plain flour
150 g (4 3/4 oz) butter,
  softened to room
  temperature
1 cup (230 g/7 1/3 oz)
  firmly packed soft
  brown sugar plus
  1 tablespoon, extra
2 eggs
1 tablespoon milk
1 teaspoon vanilla
  essence
3/4 cup (75 g/2 1/2 oz)
  walnut halves, chopped

1. Preheat the oven to
moderate 180°C
(350°F/Gas 4). Brush a
20 cm (8 inch) square
tin with melted butter
or oil and line the base
with baking paper.
2. Sift the flours
together into a bowl. In
a large bowl, beat the
butter and sugar until
light and creamy. Add
1 egg, beat well and add
1 tablespoon of the
flours. Beat in the second
egg, milk and vanilla.

Fold in the remaining
flour and 1/2 cup
(50 g/1 2/3 oz) walnuts.
Spoon into the tin and
smooth the surface.
3. Scatter the top with
the remaining chopped
walnuts and extra
brown sugar. Bake for
35–40 minutes. Cool in
the tin. Carefully turn
out and cut into
squares or rectangles.

Peanut Butter Brownies

Preparation time:
  15 minutes + cooling
Total cooking time:
  30 minutes
Makes 16

2 eggs
1 cup (250 g/8 oz)
  caster sugar
1/2 cup (115 g/3 3/4 oz)
  firmly packed soft
  brown sugar
30 g (1 oz) butter,
  softened
1/4 cup (60 g/2 oz)
  crunchy peanut butter
1 teaspoon vanilla
  essence
1 1/3 cups (165 g/
  5 1/2 oz) plain flour
2 teaspoons baking
  powder
1/3 cup (50 g/1 2/3 oz)
  roasted salted
  peanuts, chopped

1. Preheat the oven to
moderate 180°C
(350°F/Gas 4). Lightly
brush the sides and
base of a 23 cm
(9 inch) square cake
tin with melted butter
or oil. Line the base
with baking paper,
extending over 2 sides.
2. Place the eggs in a
medium bowl and beat
with electric beaters
until well combined.
Add the sugars,
softened butter, peanut
butter and vanilla. Beat
for 2–3 minutes at
medium speed. Sift
together the flour and
baking powder. Add all
at once to the mixture
and stir to combine.
Don't overbeat.
3. Transfer the mixture
to the prepared tin.
Wet your fingers and
spread the mixture
evenly in the tin; smooth
the surface. Sprinkle
evenly with the nuts,
pressing lightly into the
mixture. Bake for
30 minutes, or until a
skewer comes out clean
when inserted in the
centre. Cool in the tin
for 15 minutes before
turning out onto a wire
rack to cool. Cut into
squares or rectangles.
Can be refrigerated in
an airtight container
for up to 4 days.

Note: You can use
unsalted peanuts.

*Caramel Brownies (top) and
Peanut Butter Brownies*

Coconut Brownies

Preparation time:
  20 minutes + cooling
Total cooking time:
  35 minutes
Makes 16

100 g (3¹/₃ oz) butter
1 cup (250 g/8 oz)
  caster sugar
3 eggs
1 cup (125 g/4 oz) plain
  flour
¹/₂ cup (55 g/1³/₄ oz)
  coconut milk powder
1 teaspoon baking
  powder
1 tablespoon milk plus
  2 teaspoons, extra
¹/₄ cup (30 g/1 oz)
  cocoa powder, sifted
¹/₄ cup (25 g/³/₄ oz)
  desiccated coconut

1. Preheat the oven to moderate 180°C (350°F/Gas 4). Brush a 20 cm (8 inch) square tin with melted butter or oil and line the base with baking paper.
2. Beat the butter and sugar in a small bowl until light and creamy. Beat in the eggs, one at a time, adding 1 tablespoon of the flour after each egg — this prevents the mixture from separating. Transfer to a large bowl. Fold in the coconut milk powder and the remaining sifted flour and baking powder. Stir in the tablespoon of milk. Divide the mixture equally, placing half in another bowl.
3. Add the cocoa powder with the extra milk to one half of the mixture, folding gently to combine. Add the coconut to the other half of the mixture and fold in gently to combine.
4. Place spoonfuls of the two mixtures alternately in the base of the prepared tin. Using a knife or a skewer, swirl the mixture to make a marbled effect. Don't overmix or you'll end up with just a chocolate mixture. Smooth the top. Bake for 35 minutes or until the top feels firm when lightly pressed with your finger. A skewer inserted into the centre of the brownie mixture should come out clean.
5. Allow to cool in the tin for a few minutes and then carefully remove from the tin. Cool completely on a wire rack before cutting into squares, diamonds or rectangles.

Note: Coconut milk powder is readily available from supermarkets and speciality shops.

Date and Fig Brownies

Preparation time:
  15 minutes + cooling
Total cooking time:
  25–30 minutes
Makes 16

125 g (4 oz) butter
100 g (3¹/₃ oz) dark
  chocolate, chopped
¹/₂ cup (125 g/4 oz)
  caster sugar
¹/₄ cup (90 g/3 oz)
  golden syrup
3 eggs, lightly beaten
³/₄ cup (90 g/3 oz)
  self-raising flour
¹/₄ cup (30 g/1 oz) plain
  flour
¹/₄ cup (30 g/1 oz)
  cocoa powder
¹/₃ cup (60 g/2 oz)
  pitted and chopped
  fresh dates
¹/₄ cup (45 g/1¹/₂ oz)
  chopped soft,
  dried figs
sifted cocoa powder, for
  decoration

1. Preheat the oven to moderate 180°C (350°F/Gas 4). Brush a 28 x 18 cm (11 x 7 inch) shallow tin with melted butter or oil and line the base with baking paper.
2. Melt the butter and chocolate in a heatproof bowl, over a pan of simmering water, stirring until smooth.

Date and Fig Brownies (left) and Coconut Brownies

3. Add the sugar to the bowl, stir until almost dissolved and then add the golden syrup. Stir in the eggs and fold in the flours, cocoa powder, dates and figs. Pour into the prepared tin.
4. Bake 25–30 minutes; allow to cool in the tin. Cut into squares or cut with a shaped biscuit cutter, as shown in the picture. Dust with cocoa just before serving.

9

1. *Line the square tin with baking paper, extending over 2 sides.*

2. *Add the chocolate mixture to the egg mixture and stir with a wooden spoon.*

Two-tone Fudge Brownies

Preparation time:
15 minutes
+ cooling
Total cooking time:
40 minutes
Makes about 20

Chocolate Mixture
60 g (2 oz) butter
90 g (3 oz) dark
chocolate, roughly
chopped
1/2 cup (125 g/4 oz)
caster sugar
1 teaspoon vanilla
essence
1 egg, lightly beaten
1/2 cup (60 g/2 oz)
plain flour

White Chocolate
Mixture
60 g (2 oz) butter
90 g (3 oz) white
chocolate buttons

1/2 cup (125 g/4 oz)
caster sugar
1 teaspoon vanilla
essence
1 egg, lightly beaten
1/2 cup (60 g/2 oz)
plain flour

1. Preheat the oven to moderate 180°C (350°F/ Gas 4). Lightly brush a 20 cm (8 inch) square tin with melted butter or oil and line the base with baking paper, extending over 2 sides.
2. *To make Chocolate Mixture:* Stir the butter and chocolate in a small heatproof bowl, over a pan of simmering water, until just melted. Using a wooden spoon, beat the sugar, vanilla essence and egg in a medium bowl until combined; stir in the chocolate mixture. Add the flour, stirring until just combined; don't overbeat.

3. *To make White Chocolate Mixture:* Stir the butter and white chocolate in a small heatproof bowl, over a pan of simmering water, until just melted. Using a wooden spoon, beat the caster sugar, vanilla essence and beaten egg in a medium bowl until combined; stir in the white chocolate mixture. Add the sifted flour, stirring until just combined. Don't overbeat.
4. Drop large spoonfuls of the mixtures alternately and evenly, next to one another, in a single layer, in the tin. Gently smooth the surface, without combining the mixtures. Bake for 35 minutes, or until firm. Allow to cool in the tin before cutting into small pieces. Shown sprinkled with icing sugar.

Two-tone Fudge Brownies

3. Stir the butter and white chocolate in a heatproof bowl over simmering water.

4. Drop large spoonfuls of the mixtures, alternately, in a single layer in the tin.

Marshmallow Brownies

Preparation time:
  20 minutes + cooling
Total cooking time:
  40–45 minutes
Makes 24

150 g (4³/4 oz) butter,
  chopped
125 g (4 oz) dark
  chocolate, chopped
3 eggs
1 cup (250 g/8 oz)
  caster sugar
1 teaspoon vanilla
  essence
1 cup (125 g/4 oz) plain
  flour
¹/4 cup (30 g /1 oz)
  cocoa powder
1 cup (160 g/5¹/4 oz)
  unsalted peanuts
1 cup (45 g/1¹/2 oz)
  mini-marshmallows

1. Preheat the oven to moderate 180°C (350°F/Gas 4). Brush a 20 cm (8 inch) square cake tin with oil or melted butter. Line the base with baking paper, extending over 2 sides.
2. Stir the butter and chocolate in a heatproof bowl, over a pan of simmering water, until just melted. Remove from the heat and allow to cool slightly.
3. Beat the eggs, sugar and vanilla together in a large bowl, with a wire whisk, until well combined. Sift the flour and cocoa together. Whisk the chocolate mixture into the eggs and stir in the flour and cocoa; do not overbeat. Fold in the peanuts and marshmallows.
4. Pour into the cake tin. Bake for 40–45 minutes, until slightly risen and just firm to the touch. Cool in the tin (it will sink back down to form a flat surface) and when completely cold, lift out and cut into squares. Shown drizzled with melted dark chocolate.

Butterscotch Brownies

Preparation time:
  15 minutes + cooling
Total cooking time:
  30 minutes
Makes 20

2 eggs
2 cups (460 g/14¹/2 oz)
  firmly packed dark
  brown sugar
125 g (4 oz) butter,
  melted
1 teaspoon vanilla
  essence
1¹/2 cups (185 g/6 oz)
  plain flour
2 teaspoons baking
  powder
1 cup (140 g/4²/3 oz)
  chopped brazil nuts

1. Preheat the oven to moderate 180°C (350°F/Gas 4). Lightly brush the sides and base of a 23 cm (9 inch) square cake tin with melted butter or oil. Line the base with baking paper, extending over 2 sides.
2. Beat the eggs in a medium bowl, using electric beaters, until well combined. Add the sugar, melted butter and vanilla essence. Beat at medium speed for 2–3 minutes or until creamy. Sift together the flour and baking powder. Fold through the egg mixture with the nuts until combined. Don't overbeat.
3. Spoon the mixture into the cake tin, using a spatula to spread evenly. Smooth the surface. Bake for 30 minutes or until firm and crusty on top. Allow to cool in the tin before turning out onto a wire rack. Cut into squares or rectangles. Shown dusted with icing sugar. Can be refrigerated in an airtight container for up to 4 days.

Butterscotch Brownies (top) and Marshmallow Brownies

Peanut Brownie Cookies

Preparation time:
  15 minutes + cooling
Total cooking time:
  8–10 minutes
  + 15 minutes per batch
Makes 18

*1 cup raw peanuts,
  roughly chopped
125 g (4 oz) butter,
  softened
1 cup (250 g/8 oz)
  caster sugar
1 egg, lightly beaten
1¹/2 cups (185 g/6 oz)
  plain flour
1 teaspoon baking
  powder
2 tablespoons cocoa
  powder
¹/2 cup (90 g/3 oz) dark
  choc bits*

1. Preheat the oven to moderate 180°C (350°F/Gas 4). Spread the chopped peanuts on a baking tray, bake for 8–10 minutes until lightly golden. Set aside to cool. Lightly brush 3 baking trays with melted butter or oil and line with baking paper.
2. In a small bowl, beat the butter and sugar with electric beaters for 2–3 minutes until creamy. Gradually beat in the egg. Sift together the plain flour, baking powder and cocoa.

Using a metal spoon, fold gradually into the butter mixture, incorporating well between each addition. Stir in the peanuts and choc bits.
3. Place heaped tablespoonsful of mixture, well spaced to allow for spreading, on the prepared tray. (You will only be able to bake about 6 cookies per tray at a time.) Bake for 15 minutes — the cookies will still be a little bit soft. Leave on the tray to firm for 2–3 minutes, before transferring to a wire rack to cool.

Note: A chocolate glacé icing can be spread onto these brownie cookies. To make it, sift 1 cup (125 g/4 oz) of icing sugar with 1¹/2 tablespoons of cocoa into a small heatproof bowl. Add 15 g (¹/2 oz) of butter and stir in 1–1¹/2 tablespoons of hot water, enough to make a firm icing. Stir over a pan of simmering water until the icing is glossy and smooth. Do not overheat or it will become grainy. Spread onto the cookies with a flat-bladed knife, and decorate with some chopped roasted peanuts, if you like.

Basic Brownies

Preparation time:
  20 minutes + cooling
Total cooking time:
  40 minutes
Makes 24

*150 g (4³/4 oz) butter,
  chopped
125 g (4 oz) dark
  chocolate, chopped
3 eggs
1¹/2 cups (375 g/12 oz)
  caster sugar
1 teaspoon vanilla
  essence
1 cup (125 g/4 oz) plain
  flour
¹/4 cup (30 g /1 oz)
  cocoa powder
icing sugar, to dust*

1. Preheat the oven to moderate 180°C (350°F/Gas 4). Brush a 20 cm (8 inch) square cake tin with oil or melted butter. Line the base with baking paper, extending over 2 sides.
2. Melt the butter and the chocolate in a heatproof bowl, over a pan of simmering water, stirring occasionally. Remove from the heat and allow to cool slightly.
3. Use a wire whisk to beat the eggs, sugar and vanilla together in a large bowl until well combined. Sift the flour and cocoa together.

Peanut Brownie Cookies (above) and Basic Brownies

Whisk the chocolate mixture into the egg mixture and then stir in the sifted flour and cocoa; do not overbeat.
4. Pour into the prepared tin. Bake for 40 minutes, until slightly risen and just firm to the touch. Leave to cook in the tin (it will sink back down to form a flat surface) then lift out and cut into squares when completely cold. Dust with icing sugar to serve. The brownies in the picture have been decorated with crystallised violets.

15

Chunky Brownies

Preparation time:
  15 minutes + cooling
Total cooking time:
  40–45 minutes
Makes 16

150 g (4³/4 oz) butter
150 g (4³/4 oz) dark
  chocolate
³/4 cup (165 g/5¹/2 oz)
  firmly packed soft
  brown sugar
3 eggs
1 teaspoon vanilla
  essence
1 cup (125 g/4 oz) plain
  flour
¹/4 cup (30 g/1 oz)
  cocoa powder
¹/2 cup (50 g/1²/3 oz)
  halved walnuts
¹/2 cup (60 g/2 oz)
  raisins
50 g (1²/3 oz) milk
  chocolate, chopped

1. Preheat the oven
to moderate 180°C
(350°F/Gas 4). Brush
a 20 cm (8 inch) square
cake tin with melted
butter or oil and
line the base with
baking paper.
2. Melt the butter and
dark chocolate in a
heatproof bowl, over
a pan of simmering
water, stirring until
the mixture is smooth.

Remove from the heat
and cool slightly.
3. Add the sugar, stir
until fully dissolved and
beat in the eggs and
vanilla. Fold in the flour,
cocoa, walnuts, raisins
and chocolate and pour
into the tin. Bake for
35–40 minutes. Allow to
cool in the tin, turn out
and cut into squares.
Shown decorated with
grated chocolate.

Note: Walnuts can be
toasted briefly, on an
oven tray, in a
moderate 180°C
(350°F/Gas 4) oven,
before using.

Strawberry Brownies

Preparation time:
  15 minutes + cooling
Total cooking time:
  35–40 minutes
*Makes 16 or 8, if
  serving as a dessert*

125 g (4 oz) butter
125 g (4 oz) dark
  chocolate
¹/2 cup (125 g/4 oz)
  sugar
¹/4 cup (80 g/2²/3 oz)
  strawberry jam
2 eggs
1 teaspoon vanilla
  essence
¹/2 cup (60 g/2 oz) self-
  raising flour
¹/2 cup (60 g/2 oz)
  plain flour
fresh strawberries, for
  serving (optional)

1. Brush a 20 cm
(8 inch) square cake
tin with melted butter
or oil and line the base
with baking paper.
Preheat the oven to
moderate 180°C
(350°F/Gas 4).
2. Melt the butter and
chocolate in a
heatproof bowl.
over a pan of
simmering water,
stirring until the
mixture is smooth.
3. Add the sugar and
stir until it is almost
dissolved. Stir in the
strawberry jam and
remove from the heat.
Beat in the eggs and a
pinch of salt, add the
vanilla and fold in the
flours. Pour into the
prepared cake tin.
4. Bake for 25–30
minutes and allow to
cool in the tin before
cutting into squares.
Pictured with melted
chocolate and
strawberries. If serving
as a dessert, cut into
4 large squares, cut
each square into
2 triangles and serve
with a bowl of fresh
strawberries and
some vanilla ice
cream or cream.

*Strawberry Brownies (top) and
Chunky Brownies*

Apricot and Almond Brownies

Preparation time:
  15 minutes + cooling
Total cooking time:
  40 minutes
Makes 16

125 g (4 oz) butter
125 g (4 oz) dark
  chocolate
3 eggs
3/4 cup (185 g/6 oz)
  sugar
1 teaspoon vanilla
  essence
1/2 cup (60 g/2 oz) self-
  raising flour
1/2 cup (60 g/2 oz) plain
  flour
1/3 cup (95 g/3 1/4 oz)
  dried apricots, cut
  into slivers
1/2 cup (80 g/2 2/3 oz)
  almonds, chopped

1. Preheat the oven to
moderate 180°C
(350°F/Gas 4). Brush a
20 cm (8 inch) square
tin with melted butter
or oil and line the base
with baking paper.
2. Melt the butter and
chocolate in a heatproof
bowl, over a pan of
simmering water,
stirring until the
mixture is smooth.
3. Beat the eggs, sugar
and vanilla in a large
bowl with a wire whisk,
until just combined.
Whisk in the chocolate
mixture and stir in the
sifted flours, a pinch of
salt, apricots and
almonds. Don't overbeat.
Pour into the tin and
bake for 35 minutes.
4. Cool in the tin and
cut into squares.
Decorated with gold
leaf in the picture.

Jaffa Brownies

Preparation time:
  25 minutes + cooling
Total cooking time:
  40 minutes
Makes 24

Orange Mixture
60 g (2 oz) butter,
  softened
1 tablespoon finely
  grated orange rind
185 g (6 oz) cream
  cheese, at room
  temperature
1/4 cup (60 g/2 oz)
  caster sugar
2 eggs, lightly beaten
1/4 cup (30 g/1 oz) plain
  flour

Chocolate Mixture
185 g (6 oz) dark
  chocolate, chopped
45 g (1 1/2 oz) butter,
  chopped
2 eggs
3/4 cup (185 g/6 oz)
  caster sugar
1/2 cup (60 g/2 oz) plain
  flour
1/4 cup (30 g/1 oz) self-
  raising flour

1. Preheat the oven to
moderate 180°C
(350°F/Gas 4). Lightly
brush a 20 x 30 cm
(8 x 12 inch) lamington
tin with melted butter
or oil and line the base
with baking paper,
extending over 2 sides.
2. *To make Orange
Mixture:* In a small
bowl, using electric
beaters, beat the butter,
orange rind and cream
cheese for 2–3 minutes
until creamy. Gradually
add the caster sugar
and then the eggs, a
little at a time. Stir in
the flour and set aside.
3. *To make Chocolate
Mixture:* Melt the
chocolate and butter in
a small heatproof bowl,
over a pan of boiling
water, stirring
occasionally. Set aside
to cool. In a small
bowl, using electric
beaters, beat the eggs
and sugar for 2–3
minutes until thick and
creamy. Transfer to a
large bowl. Add the
cooled chocolate to
the bowl, stir until
combined and stir in the
combined sifted flours.
4. To assemble, pour
about two-thirds of the
Chocolate Mixture into
the prepared tin and
spread evenly. Pour the
Orange Mixture over
the top and smooth
the surface. Using a
spatula, make three

Jaffa Brownies (top) and Apricot and Almond Brownies

trenches, evenly spaced across the mixture. Pour the remaining Chocolate Mixture into the trenches. Use the spatula to cut and spread the Chocolate Mixture through the Orange Mixture, to create a marbled effect. Bake for 30 minutes, or until firm. Allow brownies to cool in the tin before cutting into pieces. Can be refrigerated in an airtight container for up to 4 days.

19

Fudge Brownies

Preparation time:
  10 minutes + cooling
Total cooking time:
  40 minutes + cooling
Makes 16

150 g (4³/4 oz) butter
200 g (6¹/2 oz) dark
  chocolate
³/4 cup (185 g/6 oz)
  caster sugar
3 eggs
1 teaspoon vanilla
  essence
1 cup (125 g/4 oz) plain
  flour, sifted

1. Preheat the oven to
moderate 180°C
(350°F/Gas 4). Brush a
20 cm (8 inch) square
tin with oil or melted
butter and line the base
with baking paper.
2. Melt the butter,
chocolate and sugar
in a heatproof bowl,
over a pan of
simmering water,
stirring occasionally.
Remove from the heat.
3. Beat in the eggs and
the vanilla, then fold in
the flour. Pour into the
prepared tin and bake
for 35 minutes.
4. Remove from the
oven and cool in the tin
before turning out and
cutting into squares.

*Fudge Brownies (top) and
Dessert Brownies*

Dessert Brownies

Preparation time:
  20 minutes
  + refrigeration
Total cooking time:
  45 minutes
Serves 6

150 g (4³/4 oz) butter
125 g (4 oz) dark
  chocolate
3 eggs
1¹/2 cups (375g/12 oz)
  caster sugar
1 teaspoon vanilla
  essence
1 cup (125g/4 oz) plain
  flour
¹/4 cup (30g/1 oz)
  cocoa powder
2 tablespoons instant
  coffee powder
vanilla ice cream

Sauce
1 cup (250 ml/8 fl oz)
  cream
200 g (6¹/2 oz) dark
  chocolate, chopped
2 tablespoons Grand
  Marnier, or to taste

1. Preheat the oven to
moderate 180°C
(350°F/Gas 4). Brush
a shallow 28 x 18 cm
(11 x 7 inch) baking tin
with oil or melted
butter; line the base
with baking paper,
extending over 2 sides.

2. Melt the butter and
chocolate in a small
heatproof bowl over
a pan of simmering
water, stirring until
smooth. Remove from
the heat and allow to
cool slightly.
3. In a large bowl,
whisk the eggs, sugar
and vanilla essence
until well combined.
Whisk in the chocolate
mixture, then stir in the
sifted flour, cocoa and
coffee powder. Do not
overbeat. Pour into
the prepared tin and
bake for 40 minutes.
Cool completely in
the tin, then refrigerate
for 1 hour or until firm.
4. *To make Sauce:*
Combine the cream
and chopped chocolate
in a small pan and heat
gently over very low
heat until the chocolate
begins to melt. Remove
from the heat and stir
until smooth. Add the
Grand Marnier and
stir to combine.
5. Lift the brownie
from the tin, using the
baking paper. Using an
8 cm (3 inch) round
biscuit cutter, cut out
6 rounds. Place each
round on a serving
plate, serve with
ice cream and drizzle
with the warm sauce.
Fancy chocolates may
be used to decorate
if you like, as shown
in the picture.

Choc-chip and Nut Brownies

Preparation time:
  20 minutes + cooling
Total cooking time:
  30 minutes
Makes 50

125 g (4 oz) butter,
  chopped
200 g (6^1/2 oz) dark
  chocolate, chopped
3 eggs
1^1/2 cups (375 g/12 oz)
  caster sugar
1 teaspoon vanilla
  essence
1^1/2 cups (185 g/6 oz)
  plain flour
^{1}/3 cup (40 g/1^1/3 oz)
  cocoa powder
1^1/2 cups (185 g/6 oz)
  chopped walnuts
1^1/2 cups (265 g/
  8^1/2 oz) dark choc bits

1. Preheat the oven to moderate 180°C (350°F/Gas 4). Brush a shallow 20 x 30 cm (8 x 12 inch) tin with oil or melted butter, and line the base with baking paper, extending over the 2 long sides.
2. Melt the butter and dark chocolate in a heatproof bowl, over a pan of simmering water, stirring occasionally.
3. Using electric beaters, beat the eggs in a large bowl for 2 minutes, until light and foamy. Add the sugar gradually, beating well after each addition. Beat in the vanilla essence.
4. Fold the chocolate mixture into the egg mixture with a metal spoon, until almost combined. Sift the flour and cocoa, fold in and then gently stir in the walnuts and choc bits until combined. Pour into the prepared tin and bake for 30 minutes. Allow to cool in the tin before cutting into pieces. Shown decorated with melted white chocolate and walnut halves.

Brownie Cookies

Preparation time:
  15 minutes
  + cooling
Total cooking time:
  12 minutes
Makes 18

1^1/2 cups (185 g/6 oz)
  plain flour
^{3}/4 cup (90 g/3 oz)
  cocoa powder
1^1/2 cups (280 g/9 oz)
  lightly packed soft
  brown sugar

185 g (6 oz) butter
150 g (4^3/4 oz) dark
  chocolate, chopped
3 eggs, lightly beaten
1 cup (175 g/5^2/3 oz)
  dark choc bits

1. Preheat the oven to moderate 180°C (350°F/Gas 4). Line 2 oven trays with baking paper.
2. Sift the flour and cocoa powder into a large bowl, add the brown sugar and make a well in the centre.
3. Melt the butter and the chocolate in a heatproof bowl over a pan of simmering water, stirring occasionally. Add to the flour mixture along with the eggs, and stir until combined. Stir in the choc bits.
4. Drop heaped tablespoonsful of the mixture onto the prepared trays, leaving room for spreading. Flatten slightly with your fingertips. Bake for 12 minutes — the cookies will still be soft. Cool on the trays for 5 minutes before transferring to a wire rack to cool.

Variation: Use white or milk chocolate bits in place of dark, if you prefer.

Brownie Cookies (top) and
Choc-chip and Nut Brownies

1. Whisk the sugar, vanilla essence and eggs into the chocolate mixture.

2. Spread the mixture into the prepared tin and smooth the surface.

Ice Cream Brownies

Preparation time:
  30 minutes + cooling
Total cooking time:
  30 minutes
Makes 6

125 g (4 oz) butter,
  chopped
185 g (6 oz) dark
  chocolate, chopped
1 cup (250 g/8 oz)
  caster sugar
2 teaspoons vanilla
  essence
2 eggs, lightly
  beaten
1 cup (125 g/4 oz)
  plain flour, sifted
1/2 cup (60 g/2 oz)
  chopped walnuts
1 litre chocolate chip
  ice cream

Fudge Sauce
100 g (3 1/3 oz) dark
  chocolate

60 g (2 oz) butter
1/2 cup (115 g/3 2/3 oz)
  firmly packed soft
  brown sugar
300 ml (9 1/2 oz) cream
1 tablespoon cocoa
  powder

1. Preheat the oven to moderate 180°C (350°F/Gas 4). Lightly brush a 20 x 30 cm (8 x 12 inch) tin with melted butter or oil. Line the base with baking paper, extending over 2 sides. Place the butter and chocolate in a medium heatproof bowl. Stand the bowl over a pan of simmering water until butter and chocolate have melted. Remove the bowl from the heat; cool slightly.
2. Whisk in the caster sugar, vanilla and eggs. Sift the flour into the bowl, stir until just combined and fold the

walnuts through. Don't overbeat. Spread into the prepared tin and smooth the surface. Bake for 30 minutes or until firm. Leave in the tin until the mixture is completely cold.
3. Soften the ice cream slightly. Spread evenly on a foil-lined tray to form a 15 x 20 cm (6 x 8 inch) rectangle. Cover and re-freeze.
4. Remove the Brownies from the tin and cut into 12 squares. Working quickly with the ice cream, cut 6 portions the same size as the Brownies. Sandwich the ice cream between the brownies, dust the tops with icing sugar and serve with the Fudge Sauce.
5. *To make Fudge Sauce:* Stir all the ingredients in a medium bowl, over a pan of simmering water, until melted and smooth.

Ice Cream Brownies

3. *Spread the ice cream evenly onto a foil-lined tray.*

4. *Remove the brownies from the tin and cut into 12 squares.*

25

Ultimate Chocolate Brownies

Preparation time:
  20 minutes
Total cooking time:
  40–45 minutes
Makes 30

1/3 cup (40 g/1 1/3 oz)
  plain flour
1/2 cup (60 g/2 oz) dark
  cocoa powder
2 cups (500 g/1 lb) sugar
1 cup (130 g/4 1/4 oz)
  chopped pecans or
  pistachios
250 g (8 oz) dark
  chocolate
250 g (8 oz) butter
2 teaspoons vanilla
  essence
4 eggs, lightly beaten

1. Preheat the oven to moderate 180°C (350°F/Gas 4). Brush a 20 x 30 cm (8 x 12 inch) cake tin with melted butter or oil. Line the base with baking paper, extending over the 2 long sides.
2. Sift the flour and cocoa into a large bowl and combine with the sugar and nuts. Mix thoroughly and make a well in the centre.
3. Use a large sharp knife to chop the chocolate into small pieces. Add the

chocolate pieces to the dry ingredients.
4. Melt the butter in a small pan over low heat. Add it to the dry ingredients, with the vanilla and eggs. Stir until the ingredients are well combined.
5. Pour the mixture into the prepared tin, smooth the surface and bake for 40–45 minutes. The mixture will still be a bit soft inside. Set aside for up to 2 hours before cutting, or refrigerate if you prefer. When set, cut into pieces. Picture shows brownies drizzled with melted chocolate and decorated with gold dragées.

Note: These brownies have a flaky, uneven surface and a rich chocolate centre. The secret of a good brownie is in the quality of the ingredients you use — the better quality chocolate and cocoa used, the more delicious the result will be. Use a good, bitter-sweet, dark cooking chocolate (sometimes known as couverture). Look for dark cocoa powder in speciality shops — Dutch is the best. They may be more expensive, but are well worth it.

Honeycomb Brownies

Preparation time:
  15 minutes + cooling
Total cooking time:
  40 minutes
Makes 16

100 g (3 1/3 oz)
  chocolate-coated
  honeycomb bars
125 g (4 oz) butter
185 g (6 oz) dark
  chocolate, chopped
2 eggs
1 cup (250 g/8 oz)
  caster sugar
2 teaspoons vanilla
  essence
1 cup (125 g/4 oz) plain
  flour, sifted

1. Preheat the oven to moderate 180°C (350°F/Gas 4). Lightly brush a 20 cm (8 inch) square tin with melted butter or oil. Line the base with baking paper, extending over 2 sides. Roughly chop the honeycomb bars. Melt the butter and chocolate in a small heatproof bowl, over a pan of simmering water, stirring occasionally.
2. Transfer the mixture to a medium bowl. Whisk in the eggs, caster sugar and vanilla essence. Add the sifted flour, stir until well incorporated and then

Ultimate Chocolate Brownies (top) and Honeycomb Brownies

fold the honeycomb through the mixture.
3. Pour into the prepared tin, pushing any exposed honeycomb into the mixture, and smooth the surface. Bake for 35 minutes, or until firm. Allow to cool in the tin before cutting into small squares to serve.

A shaped biscuit cutter can be used to cut the brownies, as shown in the picture. Refrigerate in an airtight container for up to 1 week.

Fudges

S oft and creamy, sweet indulgences that are very much appreciated when a little sugar treat is in order. Wrapped attractively, pieces of fudge are welcome as a gift or as a contribution towards fund-raising events. Fresh home-made fudge is far superior in taste and texture to any that is commercially produced.

Florentine Caramel Fudge

Preparation time:
15 minutes
Total cooking time:
18 minutes
Makes 16 pieces

*3¹/4 cups (405 g/
12²/3 oz) pure
icing sugar
3 tablespoons
desiccated coconut
1 tablespoon golden
syrup
¹/2 cup (125 ml/4 fl oz)
milk
30 g (1 oz) butter
1 teaspoon ground ginger
1 teaspoon vanilla
essence*

1. Lightly brush a 21 x 11 cm (8¹/2 x 4¹/2 inch) loaf tin with melted butter or oil. Line base with baking paper, extending over 2 sides. Place the icing sugar, 2 tablespoons coconut, golden syrup, milk, butter and ginger in a heavy-based pan. Stir over low heat without boiling until mixture is smooth and the sugar has dissolved. Brush the mixture from the sides of the pan with a wet pastry brush.
2. Bring the mixture to the boil. Boil, without stirring, for 8 minutes, or until it reaches soft-ball stage (115°C/240°F on a sugar thermometer). Cool slightly, add the vanilla and beat with electric beaters until the mixture starts to thicken and looks creamy. Pour into the tin. Smooth the surface; sprinkle with coconut. Cut when set. Can be decorated with icing or melted chocolate and silver dragées.

Florentine Caramel Fudge

Tips for Making Fudge

Making fudge may seem daunting at first,
but once you understand all the steps involved
you will feel confident enough to give it a go
and enjoy sharing the results.

Rules for making sugar syrup

Fudge is based on a sugar syrup, which is a solution of sugar in liquid. When making a sugar syrup, whether it is as simple as sugar and water or contains other ingredients, the rules remain the same.

Always stir the sugar and liquid over low heat *without boiling* until the sugar has completely dissolved.

Stir over low heat until the sugar dissolves.

If the mixture comes to the boil before all the sugar is dissolved, a crust of sugar crystals, which is hard to get rid of, will form around the edge of the pan.

Once the sugar has completely dissolved, allow the mixture to come to the boil, and *do not* stir the mixture, unless specifically instructed to in the recipe. Stirring the boiling mixture will cause it to become cloudy and crystallised, which may or may not be desirable, depending on the recipe.

Using a sugar thermometer

Boil the mixture for the full time, as specified in the recipe. Because stoves vary so much, as do interpretations of high, medium or low heat, we have given a sugar thermometer

Attach the thermometer before the mixture boils.

reading as an exact gauge. The sugar thermometer should be fixed to the pan before the mixture comes to the boil, as handling the boiling liquid can be very hazardous.

When the mercury reaches the temperature called for in the recipe,

The mixture has reached soft-ball stage.

the fudge is ready. Watch the mixture carefully towards the end of the cooking time, as it will burn quickly if left cooking too long.

The length of time the mixture cooks, and therefore the temperature it reaches in that given time, determines how the mixture will set. Sugar thermometers are the simplest, most accurate way of determining when a syrup has reached the desired stage. When the thermometer reaches 115°C (240°F), the mixture is at soft-ball stage.

Don't worry too much if you don't have a sugar thermometer, as fudge is a fairly forgiving mixture, unlike hard sweets, for which a sugar thermometer is crucial.

Another way to check for soft-ball stage is to drop a small amount of mixture into very cold water. When rolled between your thumb and index finger, it should form a soft ball.

Brushing the pan
Brushing down the sides of the pan with a wet pastry brush dissolves any crystals which have formed on the sides of the pan. It

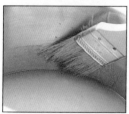

Brush any sugar crystals from sides of the pan.

is a good idea to do this if the recipe says to, but don't allow too much water to drip into the pan, as this will slow down the cooking process and interfere with the given time.

Other equipment
Heavy-based pans are best for making fudge. Because it has a high sugar content, the mixture can 'catch' and burn if the pan has a thin base, such as those on aluminium pans.

Use a long-handled wooden spoon if the mixture is to be stirred while still hot, as wood will not conduct heat.

As soon as the mixture is ready, remove the pan from the heat, place it on a wooden

Transfer the pan to a heatproof trivet.

board or heatproof trivet and allow to cool as directed. The pan will be very hot so, if it has a metal handle, use a thick cloth around the handle when moving it.

Beating the mixture
The mixture may be beaten while still hot, or you may be asked to wait until it has cooled. Beating thickens the mixture and causes it to lose its gloss. The recipe will indicate whether to

Beat mixture until it is thick and loses its gloss.

use a wooden spoon or electric beaters — it is not a good idea to use electric beaters in a very hot mixture. There is usually a fine line between the mixture reaching the desired consistency and being too firm and dry to spread into the tin, so watch it carefully as you work.

WARNING
Take great care with every step of the procedure, as hot sugar syrup is very dangerous, and the heat will transfer to any heat-conducting equipment it comes in contact with.

Keep children well away from the hot mixture.

Always use a long-handled wooden spoon for stirring.

If you do get burnt, hold the afflicted area under cold water to wash off the syrup and then keep the burn immersed in cold water for about 10 minutes.

Chocolate Fudge

Preparation time:
  15 minutes
Total cooking time:
  18 minutes
Makes 8–12 pieces

2¹/2 cups (310 g/
  9³/4 oz) pure icing
  sugar
¹/2 cup (125 ml/4 fl oz)
  milk
30 g (1 oz) butter
2 tablespoons cocoa
  powder, sifted
1 teaspoon vanilla
  essence
¹/2 cup (60 g/2 oz)
  chopped walnuts,
  optional

1. Lightly brush a 21 x
11 cm (8¹/2 x 4¹/2 inch)
loaf tin with melted
butter or oil. Line the
base with baking paper,
extending over 2 sides.
Place the icing sugar,
milk, butter and cocoa
in a medium heavy-
based pan. Stir over
low heat without
boiling until the
mixture is smooth
and the sugar has
dissolved. Brush the
mixture from the sides
of the pan with a wet
pastry brush.
2. Bring the mixture to
the boil. Boil, without
stirring, for 8 minutes,
or until it reaches soft-
ball stage (115°C/240°F
on sugar thermometer).
Allow to cool slightly,
add the vanilla and
beat with electric
beaters until the
mixture starts to
thicken and loses its
gloss. Pour into the tin,
cover and allow to set.
If using the walnuts,
press them on top when
partially set, or stir
them in before pouring
into the tin. Cut into
squares or rectangles
when set.

Vanilla Fudge

Preparation time:
  10 minutes + cooling
Total cooking time:
  25 minutes
Makes 12 pieces

2 cups (500 g/1 lb)
  caster sugar
1 cup (250 ml/8 fl oz)
  cream
1 teaspoon vanilla
  essence

1. Lightly brush a 21 x
11 cm (8¹/2 x 4¹/2 inch)
loaf tin with melted
butter or oil. Line the
base with baking paper,
extending over 2 sides.
Place the caster sugar,
cream and a pinch of
salt in a medium heavy-
based pan. Stir to
combine and continue
to stir over low heat,
without boiling, until
all the sugar has
dissolved. Increase the
heat slightly, until the
mixture is just
simmering; cover and
cook for 3 minutes.
2. Remove the lid and
clean the sugar from
the sides of the pan
with a wet pastry
brush. Do not stir the
mixture. Continue to
boil the mixture for
about 10 minutes or
until it reaches soft-ball
stage (115°C/240°F on
a sugar thermometer).
3. Remove from the
heat, allow to cool
slightly and then stir
in the vanilla essence.
Beat with electric
beaters for 1–2 minutes
or until the mixture
loses its gloss and
begins to thicken.
Quickly pour the
mixture into the
prepared tin and
smooth the surface.
Cover and allow to set.
Cut into small squares,
or use a biscuit cutter
to cut into desired
shapes. Shown here
dusted with cocoa
powder. Refrigerate for
up to 1 week.

Note: Use a good-
quality vanilla essence,
not imitation, for
the best flavour.

Vanilla Fudge (left) and Chocolate Fudge

Peanut Butter Fudge

Preparation time:
10 minutes + cooling
Total cooking time:
25 minutes
Makes 16 pieces

2 cups (500 g/1 lb)
caster sugar
3/4 cup (185 ml/6 fl oz)
cream
2 tablespoons light corn
syrup
1 teaspoon vanilla
essence
1/4 cup (60 g/2 oz)
crunchy peanut butter

1. Lightly brush a 21 x 11 cm (8^1/2 x 4^1/2 inch) loaf tin with melted butter or oil. Line the base with baking paper, extending over 2 sides. Combine the caster sugar, cream, corn syrup and a pinch of salt in a medium heavy-based pan. Stir over low heat without boiling until all the sugar has dissolved.
2. Increase the heat slightly, until the mixture is simmering. Cover and cook for another 3 minutes. Remove the lid and clean the sugar from the sides of the pan with a wet pastry brush. Do not stir the mixture. Continue to boil the mixture for 10 minutes or until it reaches soft-ball stage (115°C/240°F on sugar thermometer).
3. Remove from the heat and allow to cool slightly. Stir in the vanilla essence and peanut butter. Beat with electric beaters for 1–2 minutes or until the mixture loses its gloss and begins to thicken. Quickly pour into the tin and smooth the surface. Cover and allow to set. Cut into small squares. Picture shows fudge decorated with sprinkles. Can be refrigerated in an airtight container for up to 1 week.

Maple Nut Fudge

Preparation time:
10 minutes + cooling
Total cooking time:
15 minutes
Makes 24 pieces

2 cups (250 g/8 oz)
icing sugar, sifted
1 cup (230 g/7^1/3 oz)
firmly packed soft
brown sugar
1/4 cup (60 ml/2 fl oz)
cream
125 g (4 oz) unsalted
butter
1/2 cup (125 ml/4 fl oz)
maple syrup
1/2 cup (160 g/5 1/4 oz)
sweetened condensed
milk
1/2 cup (60 g/2 oz)
coarsely chopped
mixed nuts

1. Line the base and sides of a 20 cm (8 inch) square cake tin with aluminium foil. Brush the foil with melted butter or oil.
2. Combine the sugars, cream, unsalted butter and maple syrup in a heavy-based pan and stir over low heat until the sugars dissolve, the butter melts and the mixture is smooth. Brush the sugar crystals from the sides of the pan with a wet pastry brush.
3. Bring the mixture slowly to the boil and gradually stir in the condensed milk. Boil, without stirring, for 10 minutes, or until the mixture reaches soft-ball stage (115°C/240°F on a sugar thermometer). Remove from the heat and beat with a wooden spoon until the mixture has cooled and thickened slightly. Stir in the chopped nuts, pour into the prepared tin and leave until set.
4. Use a sharp knife to cut the fudge into small squares. Store in an airtight container.

Peanut Butter Fudge (top) and Maple Nut Fudge

We have shown the fudge decorated with tiny swirls of melted dark chocolate topped with slivered almonds. Young children will be delighted if you tell them the decorations are little bees. Put them in small coloured confectionery cases for serving at parties.

1. Stir the caster sugar, cream, salt and corn syrup with a wooden spoon.

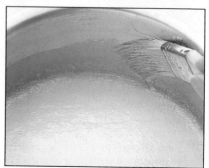

2. Use a wet pastry brush to clean the sugar from the sides of the pan.

Walnut Fudge Roll

Preparation time:
  20 minutes
  + refrigeration
Total cooking time:
28 minutes
Makes 20 pieces

1¹/2 cups (185 g/6 oz)
  walnut pieces
2 cups (500 g/1 lb)
  caster sugar
³/4 cup (185 ml/6 fl oz)
  cream
2 tablespoons light
  corn syrup
1 teaspoon vanilla
  essence

1. Place the walnut pieces on a baking tray in a moderate 180°C (350°F/Gas 4) oven for 5 minutes or until lightly toasted. Allow to cool and then chop finely. Combine the caster sugar, cream, corn syrup and a pinch of salt in a medium heavy-based pan and stir over low heat, without boiling, until all the sugar has dissolved. Brush down the sides of the pan with a wet pastry brush occasionally.
2. Increase the heat slightly, until the mixture is simmering; cover and cook for 3 minutes. Remove the lid and clean the sugar from the sides of the pan again with a wet pastry brush. Do not stir. Continue to cook, uncovered, for 10 minutes or until it reaches soft-ball stage (115°C/240°F on a sugar thermometer).
3. Remove from the heat and allow to cool slightly. Stir in the vanilla essence and one-third of the walnuts. Beat with electric beaters, until the mixture loses its gloss and begins to thicken. Turn the mixture out onto a board and, when cool enough to handle, knead gently until it just holds its shape. Don't overwork the mixture or it will become too dry. The mixture should be soft, creamy and pliable.
4. Divide the mixture in half and quickly roll each portion into a roll 20 x 5 cm (8 x 2 inches). Coat each roll evenly with the remaining walnuts (brush the rolls lightly with water, if necessary, to help the nuts stick to the fudge). Wrap each roll firmly in baking paper and refrigerate until set. Cut into slices, as shown. Keeps, refrigerated, in an airtight container for up to 1 week.

Walnut Fudge Roll

3. *Beat the fudge mixture until it loses its gloss and starts to thicken.*

4. *Lift the paper to help coat the roll evenly with the walnuts.*

Coconut Ice Fudge

Preparation time:
  15 minutes + cooling
Total cooking time:
  10 minutes
Makes 24 pieces

*2 cups (250 g/8 oz)
  icing sugar, sifted
3/4 cup (65 g/2 1/4 oz)
  desiccated coconut
1/4 cup (60 ml/2 fl oz)
  milk
1/4 cup (60 ml/2 fl oz)
  coconut milk
60 g (2 oz) butter
red food colouring
coconut flakes, for
  decorating*

1. Line the base and
sides of a 20 x 8 cm
(8 x 3 inch) loaf tin
with baking paper.
2. Combine the sugar,
coconut, milk, coconut
milk and butter in a
heavy-based pan. Stir
over medium heat until
the sugar has dissolved
and mixture is smooth.
Bring to the boil, reduce
the heat slightly and
boil, without stirring,
for about 10 minutes,
until the mixture
reaches the soft-ball
stage (115°C/240°F on
a sugar thermometer).
3. Remove from the
heat immediately
and add red colouring
until the mixture is
pale pink.

Beat until the mixture is
thick and has cooled.
Pour into the prepared
tin. Sprinkle immediately
with the extra coconut
flakes and allow to set.
4. When the fudge is
set, cut into squares
and store in an airtight
container for up to
1 week.

Million Dollar Fudge

Preparation time:
  10 minutes + cooling
Total cooking time:
  15 minutes
Makes 16 pieces

*350 g (11 1/4 oz) dark
  chocolate bits
100 g (3 1/3 oz) white
  marshmallows
2 cups (500 g/1 lb)
  caster sugar
3/4 cup (185 ml/6 fl oz)
  evaporated milk
30 g (1 oz) butter
1 teaspoon vanilla
  essence
100 g (3 1/3 oz)
  unsalted, roasted
  macadamia nuts,
  halved
1/4 cup (55 g/1 3/4 oz)
  glacé cherries,
  halved
1/4 cup (55 g/1 3/4 oz)
  glacé ginger,
  chopped*

1. Lightly brush a
20 cm (8 inch) square
tin with melted butter
or oil. Line the base
with baking paper,
extending over 2 sides.
Combine the dark
chocolate bits and
marshmallows in a
large heatproof bowl.
Set aside.
2. Stir the caster sugar,
evaporated milk and
butter in a medium
heavy-based pan until
combined. Continue
to stir over low heat
for 10 minutes or
until the sugar has
dissolved. Clean the
sugar from the sides
of the pan with a
wet pastry brush.
3. Bring the mixture to
the boil and then boil,
stirring constantly,
without touching the
sides of the pan with
the spoon, for 5 minutes
only. Quickly add the
mixture to the chocolate
and marshmallows; stir
until the chocolate melts.
4. Quickly stir through
the vanilla, nuts,
cherries and ginger.
Pour into the prepared
tin and smooth the
surface. Cover and
allow to set. Cut into
small squares. Can be
refrigerated in an
airtight container
for up to 1 week.

*Coconut Ice Fudge (top) and
Million Dollar Fudge*

Cappuccino Swirl Fudge

Preparation time:
  30 minutes
  + refrigeration
Total cooking time:
  23 minutes
Makes 20 pieces

2 cups (500 g/1 lb)
  caster sugar
1 cup (250 ml/8 fl oz)
  cream
1 teaspoon vanilla
  essence
1 teaspoon instant
  coffee powder
1 teaspoon boiling
  water

1. Lightly brush a 21 x
11 cm (8^1/2 x 4^1/2 inch)
loaf tin with melted
butter or oil. Line the
base with baking paper,
extending over 2 sides.
Place the caster sugar,
cream and a pinch of
salt in a medium
heavy-based pan
and stir to combine.
2. Stir for 10 minutes,
without boiling, over
low heat, until all the
sugar has dissolved.
Cover and cook for
3 minutes (the mixture
will begin to simmer).
Remove the lid and
clean the sugar from the
sides of the pan with a
wet pastry brush. Do
not stir the mixture.
Increase the heat slightly

and simmer, uncovered,
for about 10 minutes or
until it reaches soft-ball
stage (115°C/240°F on
sugar thermometer).
3. Remove from the
heat and allow to cool
slightly. Beat with
electric beaters for
2 minutes, or until
the mixture loses its
gloss and just begins
to thicken.
4. Quickly transfer
about one-third of the
mixture to a small bowl
and add the vanilla
essence and stir to
combine. Dissolve the
instant coffee in the
boiling water and add
to the remaining
two-thirds of the
mixture. Stir well
to combine, pour
the coffee mixture
into the prepared tin
and smooth the surface.
Place evenly spaced
spoonfuls of the
vanilla fudge over the
coffee mixture. Using
a flat-bladed knife
or a skewer, quickly
swirl the vanilla
mixture through
the coffee mixture.
5. Cover and refrigerate
for several hours, or
until firm. To serve,
cut into small squares
or use a shaped biscuit
cutter (we've used
elephant shapes). Keep
in an airtight container
in the refrigerator for
up to 1 week.

Chocolate Coconut Fudge

Preparation time:
  15 minutes + cooling
Total cooking time:
  10 minutes
Makes 15 pieces

4 cups (500 g/1 lb)
  icing sugar
150 g (4^3/4 oz) unsalted
  butter
155 ml (5 fl oz) coconut
  cream
175 g (5^2/3 oz) dark
  chocolate
1 tablespoon liquid
  glucose
^{1}/2 cup (30 g/1 oz)
  shredded coconut,
  toasted
60 g (2 oz) chocolate
  buttons, optional

1. Line the base and
sides of a 20 cm
(8 inch) square cake
tin with foil and brush
with butter or oil.
2. Combine the sugar,
butter, coconut cream,
chocolate and glucose
in a heavy-based pan.
Stir over medium heat,
without boiling, until
the sugar has dissolved,
butter has melted and
the mixture is smooth.
Bring to boil. Reduce
heat; simmer 4 minutes,
without stirring.
3. Remove from the
heat and beat with a
wooden spoon until

Chocolate Coconut Fudge (top) and Cappuccino Swirl Fudge

the mixture has cooled, thickened and lost its gloss. Stir the coconut through, pour the mixture into the cake tin and allow to set.

4. When the fudge is firm, cut it into squares but don't remove it from the tin. Melt the chocolate buttons and drizzle over the fudge,

if desired. When the chocolate has set, remove the fudge from the tin, peel away the foil and store in an airtight container.

Fruit and Nut Fudge

Preparation time:
  20 minutes + cooling
Total cooking time:
  10 minutes
Makes 40 squares

400 g (12²/3 oz) dark
  chocolate
180 g (5³/4 oz) unsalted
  butter
2 tablespoons milk
600 g (1¹/4 lb) white
  marshmallows
1–2 teaspoons vanilla
  essence
1¹/2 cups (240 g/
  7¹/2 oz) coarsely
  chopped fruit and
  nut mix

1. Line the base and
sides of a 30 x 20 cm
(12 x 8 inch) slab tin
with foil and brush
with oil.
2. Combine the
chocolate, butter, milk
and marshmallows in a
heavy-based pan and
stir over medium heat
until the marshmallows
and chocolate have
melted and the mixture
is smooth.
3. Bring to the boil,
stirring continuously,
for 1 minute. Remove
from the heat and keep
stirring until the

mixture has cooled.
Add the vanilla and
stir the mixed fruit
and nuts through.
4. Pour the mixture
into the prepared tin
and allow to set. When
firm, remove from the
tin and carefully peel
away the foil. Cut into
squares. Shown dusted
with icing sugar. Store
in an airtight container
for up to 2 weeks.

Rum and Raisin Fudge

Preparation time:
  10 minutes
Total cooking time:
  25 minutes
Makes 20 squares

2 cups (500 g/1 lb)
  caster sugar
1 cup (250 ml/8 fl oz)
  cream
1 tablespoon rum
  essence
¹/2 cup (60 g/2 oz)
  raisins, chopped

1. Lightly brush a 21 x
11 cm (8¹/2 x 4¹/2 inch)
loaf tin with melted
butter or oil. Line the
base and 2 sides with
baking paper. Combine
the caster sugar, cream
and a pinch of salt in a
medium heavy-based pan.

2. Stir to combine and
continue stirring,
without boiling, over
low heat, until all the
sugar has dissolved.
Cover and cook for
3 minutes (the mixture
will begin to simmer).
Remove the lid and
brush the sugar from the
sides of pan with a wet
pastry brush. Don't stir
the mixture. Increase the
heat slightly, and
simmer, uncovered, for
10 minutes or until it
reaches soft-ball stage
(115°C/240°F on a
sugar thermometer).
3. Remove from the
heat and allow to cool
slightly. Stir in the rum
essence. Beat with
electric beaters for
1–2 minutes or until
the mixture loses
its gloss and begins
to thicken.
4. Stir in the raisins,
pour into the tin and
smooth the surface.
Cover and allow to set.
Using a large, sharp
knife, cut the fudge into
small squares. Picture
shows fudge decorated
with shavings of white
chocolate. Keeps,
refrigerated, in an
airtight container for
up to 1 week.

Note: Rum essence is
non-alcoholic, and is
available in small
bottles from the
supermarket.

Rum and Raisin Fudge (top) and
Fruit and Nut Fudge

White Chocolate Fudge

Preparation time:
  15 minutes
  + refrigeration
Total cooking time:
  10 minutes
Makes 24 pieces

4 cups (500 g/1 lb)
  icing sugar
155 ml (5 fl oz) cream
150 g (4³/4 oz) unsalted
  butter
175 g (5²/3 oz) white
  chocolate
1 tablespoon liquid
  glucose
¹/2 cup (60 g/2 oz)
  chopped walnuts
30 g (1 oz) white
  chocolate, melted
30 g (1 oz) dark
  chocolate, melted

1. Line the base and sides of a 20 cm (8 inch) square cake tin with aluminium foil and brush the foil with butter or oil.
2. Stir the sugar, cream, butter, chocolate and glucose in a heavy-based pan over medium heat until the sugar has dissolved.
3. Bring slowly to the boil, stirring constantly. Boil 4 minutes or until golden. Keep stirring to prevent burning.
4. Remove from the heat and beat with a wooden spoon until the mixture is thick and cool. Fold in the chopped nuts.
5. Pour the mixture into the tin. Drizzle with the melted chocolates. Refrigerate for several hours to set. Cut into squares to serve. Shown sprinkled with chopped chocolate.

Russian Fudge

Preparation time:
  15 minutes
  + refrigeration
Total cooking time:
  50 minutes
Makes 36 pieces

2²/3 cups (650 g/1 lb
  5 oz) caster sugar
¹/2 cup (125 ml/
  4 fl oz) milk
125 g (4 oz) butter
200 g (6¹/2 oz)
  sweetened condensed
  milk
1 tablespoon golden
  syrup

1. Lightly brush a 20 cm (8 inch) square tin with melted butter. Line the base with baking paper, extending over 2 sides. Place the caster sugar and milk in a medium heavy-based pan. Stir to combine.
2. Place a heat pad on the burner or element. Place the pan on the heat pad, cover and bring slowly to the boil over low heat. (This will take about 20 minutes.) Brush the sugar crystals from the sides of the pan with a wet pastry brush. Add the butter, condensed milk and golden syrup to pan. Stir until mixture is smooth.
3. Boil the mixture, uncovered, for 30 minutes or until it reaches soft-ball stage (115°C/240°F on a sugar thermometer). The mixture will now be a deep caramel colour. Set aside to cool slightly and then beat with electric beaters until the fudge starts to thicken and becomes creamy. Pour into the tin, smooth the surface, cover with plastic wrap and refrigerate for several hours to set. Cut into diamonds or squares. Decorate with icing flowers if you like.

Note: Heat pads are available from hardware or kitchenware shops. This mixture will burn very easily, so if you don't have a heat pad, make sure the heat is very low.

Russian Fudge (top) and
White Chocolate Fudge

1. Boil the mixture for 5 minutes, stirring constantly.

2. Stir the chopped peppermint crisp into the mixture, using a wooden spoon.

Chocolate Mint Swirl Fudge

Preparation time:
  15 minutes
  + cooling
Total cooking time:
  10 minutes
Makes 20 pieces

4 cups (500 g/1 lb) pure
  icing sugar
155 ml (5 fl oz) cream
150 g (4³/4 oz) unsalted
  butter
225 g (7¹/4 oz)
  peppermint cream-
  filled chocolate,
  broken into pieces
1 tablespoon liquid
  glucose
2 x 35 g (1¹/4 oz)
  peppermint crisp
  bars, chopped
80 g (2²/3 oz) white
  chocolate, roughly
  chopped

1. Line a 20 cm (8 inch) square cake tin with aluminium foil and brush lightly with melted butter or oil. Combine the icing sugar, cream, butter and the peppermint cream-filled chocolate, with the glucose, in a medium heavy-based pan; stir over medium-low heat until smooth. Stirring constantly, bring the mixture slowly to the boil. Keep stirring while the mixture boils for 5 minutes.

2. Remove the pan from the heat and, use a wooden spoon to beat the mixture until it has cooled, lost its shine and has thickened slightly. Quickly stir the chopped peppermint crisp into the mixture. Pour the mixture into the prepared tin.

3. Place the white chocolate in a small heatproof bowl and stand it over a pan of barely simmering water, until softened. When soft, stir with a wooden spoon until melted and smooth. Take care not to overheat the chocolate. Drop spoonfuls of the white chocolate randomly onto the surface of the peppermint crisp mixture in the tin. Use the tip of a knife or a skewer to swirl the two mixtures together. Allow to set.

4. When the fudge is firm, remove from the tin and carefully peel away the aluminium foil. To serve, cut into squares or rectangles. The fudge will keep for up to 3 days, stored in an airtight container. Refrigerate only if the weather is very hot.

Chocolate Mint Swirl Fudge

3. Stir the white chocolate over a pan of simmering water until smooth.

4. Swirl the two mixtures together with a knife or skewer.

Hazelnut Fudge Truffles

Preparation time:
  20 minutes
  + refrigeration
Total cooking time:
  5 minutes
Makes 50 truffles

150 g (4³/4 oz) milk
  chocolate
1¹/2 tablespoons
  Grand Marnier
1/4 cup (60 ml/2 fl oz)
  cream
30 g (1 oz) butter
1³/4 cups (215 g/
  6³/4 oz) icing sugar,
  sifted
1 cup (110 g/3²/3 oz)
  ground hazelnuts
180 g (5³/4 oz) white
  chocolate

1. Stir the milk chocolate, Grand Marnier, cream and butter in a heavy-based pan over medium heat until the mixture has melted and is smooth. Transfer to a bowl.
2. Stir in the sifted icing sugar and hazelnuts in two batches. Cover and refrigerate until firm.
3. Shape teaspoonsful of mixture into balls and place on a foil-covered baking tray.
4. Melt the chocolate in a bowl over a pan of simmering water. Stir until smooth.

5. Insert a skewer into the centre of each truffle, dip each ball in the melted chocolate and allow the excess to drain off before placing on trays lined with clean foil, to set. Shown sprinkled with coconut and nuts. To serve, place the truffles in small paper or foil cases.

Note: There are a number of ways to vary truffles. Use dark chocolate instead of white, or make them two-toned, with the white inside covered with dark chocolate. Kirsch or rum or brandy can be used, along with almonds or praline. Truffles can be rolled in chocolate sprinkles or shredded coconut instead of chocolate.

Crunchy Fudge Slice

Preparation time:
  15 minutes + cooling
Total cooking time:
  5 minutes
Makes 24 pieces

250 g (8 oz) plain sweet
  biscuits
125 g (4 oz) butter
3/4 cup (90 g/3 oz) pure
  icing sugar
2 tablespoons cocoa
  powder, sifted

1/4 cup (25 g/3/4 oz)
  desiccated coconut
1/2 cup (60 g/2 oz)
  chopped pecans or
  walnuts
1/3 cup (80 g/2²/3 oz)
  chopped glacé cherries
1/3 cup (80 g/2²/3 oz)
  chopped glacé ginger
1 egg, lightly beaten
1 teaspoon vanilla
  essence

Chocolate Topping
200 g (6¹/2 oz) dark
  chocolate, chopped

1. Lightly brush a 20 x 30 cm (8 x 12 inch) tin with melted butter or oil. Line the base with baking paper, extending over the 2 long sides.
2. Crush the biscuits until fine in a food processor or place in a plastic bag and crush with a rolling pin.
3. Melt the butter in a medium heavy-based pan. Add the icing sugar and cocoa and stir over low heat for 2 minutes, or until the mixture is dissolved and smooth. Remove from the heat and stir in the biscuits, coconut, pecans or walnuts, cherries, ginger, beaten egg and vanilla essence. Stir until combined and smooth. Press into the prepared tin and smooth the surface with the base of a heavy glass.

Crunchy Fudge Slice (top) and Hazelnut Fudge Truffles

4. *To make Topping:* Place the chocolate in a small heatproof bowl and stand the bowl over a pan of barely simmering water until chocolate melts. Stir until smooth. Pour over the fudge and use a metal spatula to spread evenly. Allow to set at room temperature. Cut into small squares or rectangles. Refrigerate, covered, up to 1 week.

Toppings

O ld-fashioned favourite sauces such as chocolate, caramel and butterscotch, or new and exciting ways with fabulous fresh fruits, from cherries to bananas — they'll be eaten in a flash when served with ice cream, desserts, cakes or pancakes. Once you see how easy they are, you'll want to try them all.

Rhubarb and Orange Purée Topping

Preparation time:
  15 minutes
Total cooking time:
  10 minutes
Makes 2 cups
(500 ml/16 fl oz)

410 g (13 oz) rhubarb
1/2 cup (125 ml/4 fl oz)
  freshly squeezed
  orange juice
2–3 tablespoons caster
  sugar
4 strips orange rind,
  cut into fine slivers,
  lengthways

1. Trim the rhubarb, wash it well and then cut into 4 cm (1 1/2 inch) lengths. Cook the rhubarb and the orange juice in a small, covered pan, over gentle heat, for 5 minutes or until the rhubarb is tender. Allow to cool a little.
2. Spoon the rhubarb into a food processor, in batches if necessary, and blend until smooth. Add the sugar, to taste, pour into a jug or bowl and chill until required. (As the purée cools, it becomes thicker.)
3. Bring 1 cup (250 ml/ 8 fl oz) of water to the boil in a small pan and add the strips of orange rind. Cook for a couple of minutes or until the rind has softened and then drain.
4. Serve the purée over vanilla ice cream and top with some strips of orange rind.

Note: Wash the rhubarb thoroughly to remove any grit. Don't ever eat the leaves.

Rhubarb and Orange Purée Topping

Mixed Berry Compote

Preparation time:
  10 minutes + cooling
Total cooking time:
  20 minutes
Serves 4–6

1 cup (250 g/8 oz)
  caster sugar
1 cup (250 ml/8 fl oz)
  water
750 g (1¹/2 lb) mixed
  fresh berries
1 tablespoon
  strawberry liqueur,
  optional

1. Place the caster sugar and water in a medium heavy-based pan and stir over medium heat, without boiling, until the sugar has dissolved. Bring to the boil slowly and simmer uncovered for 10 minutes, or until the mixture has thickened to a syrupy consistency. Do not stir once the mixture is boiling.

2. Add the fresh berries to the syrup; simmer for 3–5 minutes. Make sure you do not overcook the berries as they will soften and break up.

3. Stir in the liqueur, if using, and remove the pan from the heat. Allow the compote to cool to room temperature. Serve over ice cream or with pancakes and waffles. Decorated with sugared violets in the picture.

Note: If you use strawberries and they are large, cut them half. If fresh berries are not in season, frozen berries can be used. Make sure they are thawed and drained well before adding to the syrup.

Mixed Berry Compote

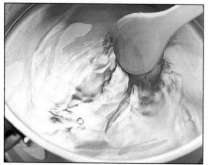

1. Stir the sugar and water over medium heat until the sugar dissolves.

2. Simmer the mixture for 10 minutes until it thickens and becomes syrupy.

3. Add the berries to the syrup and then simmer for another 3–5 minutes.

4. Add the liqueur, remove pan from the heat and allow the syrup to cool.

Hot Chocolate Sauce

Preparation time:
  5 minutes
Total cooking time:
  20 minutes
Makes about 1 1/4 cups
(315 ml/10 fl oz)

200 g (6 1/2 oz) dark
  chocolate, chopped
3/4 cup (185 ml/6 fl oz)
  water
1 tablespoon caster
  sugar
1/2 teaspoon vanilla
  essence
1/4 cup (60 ml/2 fl oz)
  cream
1 teaspoon butter
1 tablespoon rum or
  brandy, optional

1. Place the chocolate, water and sugar in the top of a double-boiler. Place over low heat and simmer until the chocolate has melted. Simmer for 15 minutes, stirring occasionally.
2. Remove from the heat, stir in the vanilla, cream, butter and rum or brandy and serve. Pictured with ice cream. Store for up to 2 weeks in a screw top jar. The sauce will thicken on refrigeration, but can be reheated gently to serve.

Fresh Fruit Sauce

Preparation time:
  5 minutes + cooling
Total cooking time:
  7 minutes
Makes about 1 cup
(250 ml/8 fl oz)

Basic Syrup
1 1/2 cups (375 g/12 oz)
  caster sugar
1 cup (250 ml/8 fl oz)
  water

200 g (6 1/2 oz) puréed
  fruit of choice such
  as strawberries,
  raspberries, kiwi
  fruit, boysenberries,
  passionfruit pulp
  including seeds, or
  poached and puréed
  nectarines, peaches
  or apricots

1. Stir the sugar and water in a small heavy-based pan over low heat without boiling until the sugar has dissolved. Brush the sugar crystals from the sides of the pan with a wet pastry brush. Boil the syrup for 2 minutes without stirring. Set aside to cool.
2. Sweeten the fruit with the cooled syrup. You will need about 2–4 tablespoons of syrup to 200 g (6 1/2 oz)

puréed fruit, depending on the desired sweetness.

Note: Refrigerate the sugar syrup in an airtight jar for up to 1 month. However, the sweetened fruit will only keep for 1 day. Serve with ice cream, desserts, cakes or, as shown, with pancakes.

Mocha Sauce

Preparation time:
  10 minutes
Total cooking time:
  5 minutes
Makes 2 cups
(500 ml/16 fl oz)

60 g (2 oz) butter
150 g (4 3/4 oz) dark
  chocolate, chopped
1 1/2 cups (375 ml/
  12 fl oz) cream
1 tablespoon instant
  coffee powder
2 tablespoons Crème
  de Cacao, optional

1. Combine the butter, chopped chocolate, cream and coffee powder in a pan. Stir over low heat until the butter and chocolate have melted and the mixture is smooth.
2. Remove from the heat and stir in the Crème de Cacao, if using. Serve warm. Shown with pastries.

From top: Mocha Sauce; Hot Chocolate Sauce;
Fresh Fruit Sauce

Honey and Nut Topping

Preparation time:
  5 minutes
Total cooking time:
  10 minutes
*Makes about 1 cup
(250 ml/8 fl oz)*

*1/4 cup (30 g/1 oz)
  slivered almonds
45 g (1 1/2 oz) unsalted
  butter
2 teaspoons cornflour
3/4 cup (260 g/8 1/3 oz)
  honey
1 teaspoon finely grated
  orange rind
1/4 cup (60 ml/2 fl oz)
  orange juice*

1. Place the slivered almonds on a sheet of foil and place under a moderately hot grill. Toast the almonds until just lightly coloured and set aside to cool.
2. Melt the butter in a small pan, over low heat, and then blend in the cornflour with a wooden spoon. Stir in the honey and bring the mixture slowly to the boil. Allow to simmer for 3–4 minutes or until the mixture has slightly thickened. Add the orange rind, orange juice and almonds and stir for another minute. Remove from the

heat and serve at once. Shown with ice cream and biscuits.

Note: Refrigerate any leftover topping in an airtight jar for up to 2 weeks. Topping thickens on refrigeration. May be gently reheated in a pan or microwave.

Caramel Sauce

Preparation time:
  5 minutes
Total cooking time:
  20 minutes
*Makes about 2 cups
(500 ml/16 fl oz)*

*1 cup (250 g/8 oz)
  caster sugar
1/4 cup (60 ml/2 fl oz)
  cold water
1/2 cup (125 ml/4 fl oz)
  hot water
400 g (12 2/3 oz)
  condensed milk
1 tablespoon golden
  syrup
1 teaspoon vanilla
  essence*

1. Stir the sugar and cold water in a small heavy-based pan over low heat, without boiling, for 10 minutes or until the sugar has dissolved. Brush any crystals from the sides of the pan with a wet pastry brush.
2. Increase the heat to

medium and simmer, without stirring, until the mixture turns a deep-coloured caramel. Remove from the heat and, with protected hands, slowly and carefully pour on the hot water. The hot caramel will spit when the hot water is added, so take care.
3. Return to low heat and stir until the caramel re-melts. Remove from the heat, stir in the condensed milk, golden syrup and vanilla essence. Serve the sauce with ice cream, pancakes or with steamed puddings and cakes. Shown with pudding and flaked almonds. Refrigerate in an airtight jar for up to 2 weeks. The sauce thickens on refrigeration.

Baked Banana Topping

Preparation time:
  10 minutes
Total cooking time:
  20 minutes
Serves 4

*30 g (1 oz) butter
1 tablespoon soft
  brown sugar
1/4 teaspoon allspice
1 tablespoon rum
4 large bananas
juice of 1 lime*

From top: Honey and Nut Topping; Baked Banana Topping; Caramel Sauce

1. Preheat the oven to moderately hot 200°C (400°F/Gas 6). Melt the butter in a small pan and add the sugar, allspice and rum.

Cook the mixture until the sugar has dissolved. **2.** Peel the bananas, cut into chunks and place in an ovenproof dish. Pour the butter mixture

over the bananas. **3.** Bake for 15 minutes, remove and pour the lime juice over the top. Shown with ice cream and slices of lime.

Mulled Black Cherry Topping

Preparation time:
  5 minutes
Total cooking time:
  25 minutes
Serves 4–6

4 cloves
1 lemon, cut into
  quarters
2 x 425 g (13¹/2 oz)
  cans black cherries
  in syrup
2 cinnamon sticks
¹/4 cup (60 ml/2 fl oz)
  brandy
4 long strips of orange
  rind about 2 cm
  (³/4 inch) wide, cut
  into matchstick-width
  strips

1. Insert a clove into each lemon quarter. Place them in a pan with the cherries and syrup, cinnamon sticks, brandy and orange rind. Bring to the boil and then reduce the heat.
2. Simmer the mixture for 20 minutes, uncovered, allowing the syrup to reduce to a thick sauce.
3. Remove and discard the lemon quarters and cloves. Serve warm or at room temperature, with vanilla ice cream.

Chocolate Rum Sauce

Preparation time:
  10 minutes
Total cooking time:
  10 minutes
*Makes about 1 cup
  (250 ml/8 fl oz)*

¹/4 cup (60 ml/2 fl oz)
  milk
¹/2 cup (125 ml/4 fl oz)
  water
30 g (1 oz) butter
60 g (2 oz) chocolate,
  chopped
1 cup (250 g/8 oz)
  caster sugar
¹/4 cup (30 g/1 oz)
  cocoa powder, sifted
1–2 tablespoons rum

1. In a small pan, stir the milk, water, butter and chocolate over low heat until butter and chocolate have melted. Add the caster sugar and cocoa powder and whisk ingredients over low heat for about 5 minutes, until the sugar has dissolved.
2. Increase the heat until the mixture reaches a low simmer and cook for 3 minutes, without boiling.
3. Remove from heat, cool for 2–3 minutes and stir in the rum.

Note: Keeps in an airtight jar for up to 2 weeks. Sauce thickens on refrigeration. Delicious with ice cream or with chocolate cake, as shown.

Butterscotch Topping

Preparation time:
  5 minutes
Total cooking time:
  15 minutes
*Makes about 1¹/2 cups
  (375 ml/12 fl oz)*

125 g (4 oz) butter
¹/2 cup (115 g/3²/3 oz)
  firmly packed soft
  brown sugar
2 tablespoons golden
  syrup
¹/2 cup (125 ml/4 fl oz)
  cream
1 teaspoon vanilla
  essence

1. Stir the butter and sugar in a pan over low heat until butter melts and sugar dissolves. Bring to the boil.
2. Add the golden syrup and cream to pan, reduce the heat; simmer for 10 minutes or until sauce has slightly thickened. Remove from heat; add the vanilla. Serve hot or at room temperature. Sauce will thicken as it cools. Shown with a profiterole and ice cream.

---

*From top: Mulled Black Cherry Topping;
Butterscotch Topping; Chocolate Rum Sauce*

Tropical Topping

Preparation time:
  10 minutes + cooling
Total cooking time:
  15 minutes
Makes 2 cups
(500 ml/16 fl oz)

1 cup (40 g/1$^{1}/_3$ oz)
  shredded coconut
2 tablespoons palm
  sugar
$^{3}/_4$ cup (185 ml/6 fl oz)
  lime juice
$^{2}/_3$ cup (125 g/4 oz)
  pawpaw, finely diced
$^{2}/_3$ cup (125 g/4 oz)
  pineapple, finely diced
$^{2}/_3$ cup (125 g/4 oz)
  mango, finely diced

1. Preheat the oven to
moderate 180°C
(350°F/Gas 4). Spread
the coconut on a
baking tray and toast in
the oven for 5–6
minutes, or until
golden. Halfway
through cooking, toss
the coconut so that it
browns evenly. Don't
let it burn.
2. In a small pan, gently
heat the palm sugar and
lime juice until the sugar
dissolves. Allow to cool;
pour over the combined
fruit. If not required
immediately, chill.
3. Spoon the topping
over ice cream and
sprinkle with the
toasted coconut.

Mango, Honey and Lime Topping

Preparation time:
  15 minutes
  + refrigeration
Total cooking time:
  16 minutes
Makes 2 cups
(500 ml/16 fl oz)

$^{1}/_4$ cup (60 ml/2 fl oz)
  water
3 tablespoons sugar
fine strips of rind from
  1 lime
1 tablespoon honey
$^{1}/_4$ cup (60 ml/2 fl oz)
  fresh lime juice
2 x 425 g (13$^{1}/_2$ oz)
  cans mango slices,
  drained, finely diced

1. Combine the water
and sugar in a small
pan and stir over low
heat without boiling
until the sugar has
dissolved. Add the lime
zest, cover and simmer
over very gentle heat
for approximately
10 minutes.
2. Remove from the
heat and cool slightly.
Add the honey and lime
juice and stir well. Pour
into a bowl; chill.
3. When ready to serve,
stir the mango through
and spoon the sauce
over ice cream.

Spiced Apple Topping

Preparation time:
  15 minutes
Total cooking time:
  15 minutes
Serves 4–6

$^{1}/_2$ cup (125 ml/4 fl oz)
  water
$^{1}/_2$ cup (125 ml/4 fl oz)
  red wine
2 tablespoons caster
  sugar
1 cinnamon stick
1 teaspoon mixed spice
1 wide strip lemon rind,
  white pith removed
4 green apples

1. Combine the water,
wine and sugar in a pan.
Stir over a low heat
without boiling until the
sugar has completely
dissolved. Add the
cinnamon stick, mixed
spice and lemon rind.
2. Peel and core the
apples, cut into thin
slices and add to the
pan. Bring to the boil,
reduce the heat slightly
and simmer, uncovered,
for 15 minutes, until the
apples are tender but
still hold their shape.
3. Cool to room
temperature and serve
apple and its liquid
with vanilla ice cream.

From top: Tropical Topping; Mango, Honey and Lime Topping; Spiced Apple Topping

Lemon, Lime and Vodka Sauce

Preparation time:
  15 minutes + cooling
Total cooking time:
  10 minutes
Serves 4–6

1 cup (250 g/8 oz)
  caster sugar
1 cup (250 ml/8 fl oz)
  water
1/4 cup (60 ml/2 fl oz)
  lemon juice
1/4 cup (60 ml/2 fl oz)
  lime juice
2 tablespoons vodka
1 tablespoon chopped
  mint
rind 1 lemon, cut in
  fine strips

1. Stir the sugar, water, lemon and lime juice in a pan over low heat until the sugar has dissolved. Bring to the boil slowly and then simmer, without stirring, until the mixture has thickened to a syrupy consistency.
2. Remove from the heat, add the vodka and set aside to cool.
3. Add the chopped mint and strips of lemon rind, pour into a sterilized jar and store in the refrigerator for up to 2 weeks.

Serve over fresh fruit such as peeled and sliced oranges or use as a poaching liquid for fruit.

Note: To make thin strips of lemon rind, either use a zester or peel wide strips of rind with a vegetable peeler. Remove all the white pith and shred the yellow rind into thin strips. If using this syrup as a poaching liquid, you may have to add a little more water before poaching. You can also use the syrup to make cocktails or simply add soda water or water for a delightfully refreshing summer drink.

Fudge Sauce with Crunchy Nuts

Preparation time:
  5 minutes
Total cooking time:
  15 minutes
*Makes 1 3/4 cups
(440 ml/14 fl oz)*

1/2 cup (80 g/2 2/3 oz)
  unsalted nuts
400 g (12 2/3 oz) can
  sweetened condensed
  milk
200 g (6 1/2 oz) dark
  chocolate
1 teaspoon vanilla
  essence

1. Preheat the oven to moderately hot 200°C (400°F/Gas 6). Roughly chop the nuts, or leave them whole if you prefer, and scatter them on a baking tray. Roast for approximately 10 minutes, stirring occasionally to ensure even browning. Be careful not to burn them. Remove from the oven and set aside to cool completely.
2. Pour the condensed milk into a heatproof bowl, break the dark chocolate into pieces and add to the bowl. Stand the bowl over a pan of simmering water, stirring until melted and smooth. Add the vanilla essence and stir thoroughly.
3. To serve, pour the hot sauce over vanilla ice cream and scatter with the roasted nuts. Picture shows plain wafers served with the ice cream.

Note: Use your favourite nuts or a combination of almonds, pecans macadamia, hazelnuts or peanuts up to the weight given.

*Lemon, Lime and Vodka Sauce (top) and
Fudge Sauce with Crunchy Nuts*

Index